This book is dedicated to Mrs. Johnson.

Jennifer Jones

Well for us, me and my fellow glues,
That's exactly what it's like
Which is why we got together
And decided we needed to go on strike!

We decided to tiptoe over to the paper pile
And grab one of the teacher's pens.
We wrote out all our grievances in a letter
And hoped that soon the abuse would end.

The worst is when you decide to taste us
Because of our scent and color.
I guess sometimes we look like a marshmallow,
And you want to have us as supper.

The kids didn't notice at first,
Not until they sat down at their desks.
They started working without us - glues,
Trying to do their best.

But then they really needed some stuff to stick
And the directions called for glue,
So they looked around the classroom for us,
But they didn't have a clue.

Then, the students grabbed some pens and paper,
And they wrote back to us as a class.
"Glues, we promise not to mistreat you anymore
If only you'll come back.

Made in United States
North Haven, CT
30 October 2022